Marriage

ALTARED STATES

Marriage

Contents

Introduction

Marriages may be made in heaven, but they occur here on earth. That fact has been the inspiration for wits throughout history. Gathered here are quotes, anecdotes, and aphorisms on the subject of matrimony—its trials, its tribulations, and its ultimate rewards. To what did Robert Mitchum attribute the length of his mar-

riage? How did Oscar Wilde describe the
effects of marriage on women? What was
Groucho Marx's definition of a wife?

These and other views on marriage have
been distilled into this handy volume. Give
it to someone you love. Or give it to your
spouse.

Only kidding!

Marriage

By all means marry; if you get a good wife, you'll be happy. If you get a bad one, you'll become a philosopher.

—Socrates

Marriageable girls as well as mothers understand the terms and perils of the lottery called wedlock. That is why women weep at a wedding and men smile.

—Honoré de Balzac

Newlyweds

· · · · · · · · · ·

Marry in haste; repent at your leisure.

—WILLIAM CONGREVE

Marriage is a great institution, but I'm not ready for an institution.

—MAE WEST

Propinquity does it.

—MRS. HUMPHREY WARD

Marriage
· · · · · · · ·

Marriage is a fight to the death. Before
contracting it, the two parties concerned
implore the benediction of Heaven,
because to promise to love each other
forever is the rashest of enterprises.

—HONORÉ DE BALZAC

Marriage is an adventure, like going to war.

—G. K. CHESTERTON

Newlyweds
· · · · · · · · · ·

Both in the lower and the middle classes
the wise-acres urge young men "to think it
over" before taking the decisive step. Thus
they foster the delusion that the choice of
a wife or husband may be governed by a
certain number of accurately weighable
pros and cons. This is a crude delusion on
the part of common sense.

—Denis de Rougemont

Marriage
· · · · · · · ·

Only choose in marriage a woman whom
you would choose as a friend if she were
a man.

—JOSEPH JOUBERT

My advice to girls: first, don't smoke—
to excess; second, don't drink—to excess;
third, don't marry—to excess.

—MARK TWAIN

I feel sure that no girl could go to the altar,
and would probably refuse, if she knew all.

—QUEEN VICTORIA

Newlyweds
· · · · · · · · ·

I was married by a judge. I should have asked for a jury.

—GEORGE BURNS

Always get married in the morning. That way, if it doesn't work out, you haven't wasted a whole day.

—MICKEY ROONEY

Men are April when they woo, December when they wed: Maids are May when they are maids, but the sky changes when they are wives.

—WILLIAM SHAKESPEARE

Marriage
· · · · · · · ·

Whoso findeth a wife findeth a good thing.

—PROVERBS 18:22

A man in the house is worth two in the street.

—MAE WEST

Keep your eyes wide open before marriage, half shut afterwards.

—BENJAMIN FRANKLIN

Newlyweds

. . . .

When a woman gets married it's like jump-
ing into a hole in the ice in the middle of
winter: You do it once, and you remember
it the rest of your days.

—MAXIM GORKY

Maidens! Why should you worry in
choosing whom you shall marry?
Choose whom you may, you will find
you have got somebody else.

—JOHN HAY

Marriage
· · · · · · · ·

Marriage is a good deal like a circus: There is not as much in it as is represented in the advertising.

—EDGAR WATSON HOWE

Marriage can be compared to a cage: Birds outside it despair to enter, and birds within, to escape.

—MICHEL DE MONTAIGNE

Newlyweds

. . . .

'Tis safest in matrimony to begin with a
little aversion.

—RICHARD BRINSLEY SHERID

Most people marry upon mingled motives,
between convenience and inclination.

—DR. JOHNSON

To take a wife merely as an agreeable and
rational companion, will commonly be
found to be a grand mistake.

—LORD CHESTERFIELD

Marriage
· · · · · · ·

All tragedies are finish'd by a death,
All comedies are ended by a marriage.

—GEORGE GORDON, LORD BYRON

Love is blind, but marriage restores its
sight.

—GEORG CHRISTOPH LICHTENBERG

You can't change a man, no-ways. By the
time his Mummy turns him loose and he
takes up with some innocent woman and
marries her, he's what he is.

—MARJORIE KINNAN RAWLINGS

Newlyweds
· · · · · · · · · ·

When a girl marries, she exchanges the attentions of many men for the inattention of one.

—HELEN ROWLAND

When an old man marries, death laughs.

—GERMAN PROVERB

The trouble with some women is that they get all excited about nothing—and then marry him.

—CHER

Marriage

· · · · · · · ·

When two people love each other, they don't look at each other, they look in the same direction.

—GINGER ROGERS

My most brilliant achievement was my ability to persuade my wife to marry me.

—WINSTON CHURCHILL

Newlyweds

· · · · · · · · ·

One of the best things about marriage is
that it gets young people to bed at a
decent hour.

—M. M. MUSSELMAN

They gave each other a smile with a future
in it.

—RING LARDNER

Children aren't happy
with nothing to ignore,
And that's what parents
were created for.

—OGDEN NASH

Married with Children

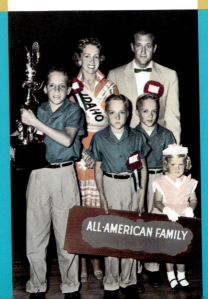

ALL-AMERICAN FAMILY

Marriage

· · · · · · · ·

Familiarity breeds contempt—and
children.

—MARK TWAIN

Women who miscalculate are called
"mothers."

—ABIGAIL VAN BUREN

Death and taxes and childbirth! There's
never any convenient time for any of them.

—MARGARET MITCHELL

Nervous breakdowns are hereditary. We get them from our children.

—Graffito

You should have seen what a fine-looking man he was before he had children.

—Arapesh Tribesman

Marriage
· · · · · · · ·

Parents are not interested in justice; they
are interested in quiet.

—BILL COSBY

The thing that impresses me most about
America is the way parents obey their
children.

—KING EDWARD VIII

Married with Children

· · · · · · · · · · · · · · · ·

The value of marriage is not that adults
produce children, but that children
produce adults.

—PETER DE VRIES

Parenthood remains the single greatest
preserve of the amateur.

—ALVIN TOFFLER

Marriage
. . . .

People who say they sleep like a baby
usually don't have one.

—Leo Burke

Before I got married I had six theories on
children; now I have six children and no
theories.

—John Wilmot

Thank God kids never mean well.

—Lily Tomlin

"Are you lost, daddy?" I asked tenderly.
"Shut up," he explained.

—RING LARDNER

Marriage

· · · · · · · ·

There are two ways to travel, first class or
with children.

—ROBERT BENCHLEY

A vacation frequently means that the family
goes away for a rest, accompanied by a
mother who sees that they all get it.

—MARCELENE COX

Cleaning your house while the kids are still growing is like shoveling the walk before it stops snowing.

—Phyllis Diller

As a housewife, I feel that if the kids are still alive when my husband gets home from work, then, hey, I've done my job.

—Roseanne Barr

Marriage

· · · · · · · ·

Children today are tyrants. They contradict
their parents, gobble their food, and
tyrannize their teachers.

—SOCRATES

The boy, of all wild beasts, is the most
unmanageable.

—PLATO

Never raise your hand at your children—
it leaves your midsection unprotected.

—ROBERT ORBEN

The fundamental defect of fathers is that they want their children to be a credit to them.

—BERTRAND RUSSELL

A father is a banker provided by nature.

—FRENCH PROVERB

The reason grandparents and grandchildren get along so well is that they have a common enemy.

—SAM LEVENSON

Marriage is the aftermath of love.

—NOEL COWARD

Homefires

Marriage
· · · · · · · ·

It is better to dwell in a corner of the
housetop, than with a brawling woman
in a wide house.

—PROVERBS

Every one of you hath his particular plague,
and my wife is mine; and he is very happy
who hath this only.

—PITTACUS *(from Plutarch)*

No matter how happily a woman may be married, it always pleases her to discover that there is a nice man who wishes she were not.

—H. L. MENCKEN

Wives are people who feel they don't dance enough.

—GROUCHO MARX

Marriage

· · · · · · · ·

Alfred, Lord Tennyson, was discussing a
particularly unhappy marriage with another
acquaintance of the couple. The marriage
was a pity, said Tennyson's companion,
because with any other spouse either of the
two unfortunates might have been happy.
"By any other arrangement," Tennyson
replied, "four people would have been
unhappy instead of two."

Spouses are impediments to great
enterprises.

—FRANCIS BACON

I have known more men destroyed by the
desire to have wife and child and to keep
them in comfort than I have seen destroyed
by drinks and harlots.

—W.B. YEATS

Marriage must incessantly contend with a monster that devours everything: familiarity.

—HONORÉ DE BALZAC

It is easier to be a lover than a husband for the simple reason that it is more difficult to be witty every day than to produce the occasional bon mot.

—HONORÉ DE BALZAC

Margaret Thatcher's husband, Dennis, was once asked who wore the pants in his family. "I do," he replied. "And I also wash and iron them."

A man in love is incomplete until he is married. Then he is finished.

—Zsa Zsa Gabor

A man marries to have a home, but also because he doesn't want to be bothered with sex and all that sort of thing.

—W. SOMERSET MAUGHAM

The only thing that holds a marriage together is the husband being big enough to step back and see where the wife is wrong.

—ARCHIE BUNKER

In marriage a man becomes slack and selfish and undergoes a fatty degeneration of the spirit.

—ROBERT LOUIS STEVENSON

Before marriage, a man declares that he would lay down his life to serve you; after marriage, he won't even lay down his newspaper to talk to you.

—HELEN ROWLAND

My wife doesn't care what I do when I'm away, as long as I don't have a good time.

—LEE TREVINO

Marriage
. . . .

You can bear your own faults, and why not
a fault in your wife?

—BENJAMIN FRANKLIN

I am glad I am not a man, for if I were,
I'd be obliged to marry a woman.

—MADAME DE STAËL

The female of the species is more deadly
than the male.

—RUDYARD KIPLING

Marriage resembles a pair of shears, so joined that they cannot be separated; often moving in opposite directions, yet always punishing anyone who comes between them.

—SYDNEY SMITH

The critical period in matrimony is breakfast time.

—PHYLLIS DILLER

Marriage may often be a stormy lake, but celibacy is almost always a muddy horse-pond.

—THOMAS LOVE PEACOCK

Marriage

. . . .

A good marriage is that in which each
appoints the other guardian of his solitude.

—RAINER MARIA RILKE

A light wife doth make a heavy husband.

—WILLIAM SHAKESPEARE

In matters of religion and matrimony I
never give any advice, because I will not
have anybody's torments in this world or
the next laid to my charge.

—LORD CHESTERFIELD

Marriage
· · · · · · · ·

It destroys one's nerves to be amiable
every day to the same human being.

> —BENJAMIN DISRAELI

A different taste in jokes is a great strain
on the affections.

> —GEORGE ELIOT

A married couple are well suited when
both partners usually feel the need for
a quarrel at the same time.

> —JEAN ROSTAND

AN OLD MAN HE COURTED ME

He comes to bed at midnight,
His feet are cold as clay,
His feet are cold as midnight,
As any corpse you say.
His joints are out of order,
His pipes are all of one tune.
I wish to God he had a-been dead
And a young man in his room.

—TRADITIONAL ENGLISH FOLK BALLAD

Marriage

· · · · · · · ·

Men have a much better time of it than
women; for one thing they marry later;
for another they die earlier.

—H.L. MENCKEN

Bachelors should be heavily taxed. It's not
fair that some men should be happier than
others.

—OSCAR WILDE

A man who wants a happy marriage should learn to keep his mouth shut and his checkbook open.

—GROUCHO MARX

Only two things are necessary to keep one's wife happy. One is to let her think she is having her own way, and the other, to let her have it.

—LYNDON B. JOHNSON

Marriage

· · · · · · · ·

A husband is what is left of the lover after
the nerve has been removed.

—HELEN ROWLAND

The majority of husbands remind me of an
orangutan trying to play the violin.

—HONORÉ DE BALZAC

I think every woman is entitled to a middle
husband she can forget.

—ADELA ROGERS ST. JOHN

Homefires

. . . .

Why does a woman work ten years to
change a man's habits and then complain
that he's not the man she married?

—BARBRA STREISAND

Many a man owes his success to his first
wife and his second wife to his success.

—JIM BACKUS

My toughest fight was my first wife.

—MUHAMMAD ALI

Man and wife make one fool.

—BEN JOHNSON

Golden Years

Marriage

· · · · · · · ·

The actress Dame Sybil Thorndike was
married to another actor, Sir Lewis Casson.
After his death, Dame Thorndike was
asked whether the couple had ever
considered divorce. "Divorce?" she said.
"Never. But murder, often!"

Golden Years

. . . .

BARBARA WALTERS: You've been married forty-two years. What makes your marriage work?

ROBERT MITCHUM: Lack of imagination, I suppose.

Marriage
. . . .

Marriage is the permanent conversation between two people who talk over everything and everyone until death breaks the record.

—CYRIL CONNOLLY

Marriage is like paying an endless visit in your worst clothes.

—J.B. PRIESTLEY

Golden Years
· · · · · · · · · ·

Even the God of Calvin never judged
anyone as harshly as married couples
judge each other.

—WILFRID SHEED

One was never married, and that's his hell;
another is, and that's his plague.

—ROBERT BURTON

Marriage
· · · · · · · ·

We study ourselves three weeks, we love each other three months, we squabble three years, we tolerate each other thirty years, and then the children start all over again.

—HIPPOLYTE TAINE

We would have broken up except for the children. Who were the children? Well, she and I were.

—MORT SAHL

Golden Years

Marriage from Love, like vinegar from wine—A sad, sour, sober beverage—by Time Is sharpened from its high celestial flavour Down to a very homely household savour.

—George Gordon, Lord Byron

Marriage

· · · · · · · ·

Wives are young men's mistresses,
companions for middle age, and old men's
nurses.

—FRANCIS BACON

One should never know too precisely
whom one has married.

—FRIEDRICH NIETZSCHE

The only reason I took up jogging was so
that I could hear heavy breathing again.

—ERMA BOMBECK

Golden Years

· · · · · · · · · ·

Marriage is the perfection which love
aimed at, ignorant of what it sought.

—RALPH WALDO EMERSON

There is nothing nobler or more admirable
than when two people who see eye to eye
keep house as man and wife, confounding
their enemies and delighting their friends.

—HOMER

Marriage
. . . .

A gentleman who had been very unhappy
in marriage, married immediately after his
wife died: Johnson said, it was the triumph
of hope over experience.

—Dr. Johnson,
quoted by James Boswell

There is so little difference between
husbands you might as well keep the first.

—Adela Rogers St. John

Golden Years

. . . .

There isn't a wife in the world who has not taken the exact measure of her husband, weighed him and settled him in her own mind, and knows him as well as if she had ordered him after designs and specifications of her own.

—CHARLES DUDLEY WARNER

I married beneath myself. All women do.

—LADY ASTOR

Marriage

· · · · · · · ·

There is no more lovely, friendly, and charming relationship, communion, or company than a good marriage.

—MARTIN LUTHER

When marrying, one should ask oneself this question: Do you believe that you will be able to converse well with this woman into your old age?

—FRIEDRICH NIETZSCHE

In marriage do thou be wise: Prefer the
person before money, virtue before beauty,
the mind before the body; then thou hast a
wife, a friend, a companion, a second self.

—WILLIAM PENN

Love seems the swiftest, but it is the
slowest of all growths. No man or woman
really knows what perfect love is until they
have been married a quarter of a century.

—MARK TWAIN

Marriage

· · · · · · · ·

Twenty years of romance make a woman look like a ruin; but twenty years of marriage make her something like a public building.

—OSCAR WILDE

Mahatma Gandhi was what women wish their husbands were: thin, tan, and moral.

—ANONYMOUS

Golden Years
· · · · · · · · · ·

American women expect to find in their husbands a perfection that English women only hope to find in their butlers.

—W. SOMERSET MAUGHAM

A man should be taller, older, heavier, uglier, and hoarser than his wife.

—EDGAR WATSON HOWE

Marriage

· · · · · · · ·

What is instinct? It is the natural tendency in one, when filled with dismay, to turn to his wife.

—FINLEY PETER DUNNE

One of the best hearing aids a man can have is an attentive wife.

—GROUCHO MARX

A good husband should always bore his
wife.

—FRED JACOB

An ideal wife is one who remains faithful
to you but tries to be just as if she weren't.

—SACHA GUITRY

Absence sharpens love; presence strengthens it.

—THOMAS FULLER

Chains do not hold a marriage together. It is threads, hundreds of tiny threads, which sew people together through the years.

—SIMONE SIGNORET

Golden Years

· · · · · · · · · ·

Marriage is the deep, deep peace of the
double bed after the hurly-burly of the
chaise longue.

—MRS. PATRICK CAMPBELL

Any marriage, happy or unhappy, is
infinitely more interesting and significant
than any romance, however passionate.

—W.H. AUDEN

Marriage
. . . .

It was an unspoken pleasure, that having come together so many years, ruined so much and repaired a little, we had endured.

—LILLIAN HELLMAN

The love we have in our youth is superficial compared to the love that an old man has for his old wife.

—WILL DURANT

Golden Years
· · · · · · · · · ·

A lady of forty-seven who has been
married twenty-seven years and has six
children knows what love really is and
described it for me like this: "Love is what
you've been through with somebody."

—James Thurber

Marriage

· · · · · · · ·

At the end of what is called the "sexual life," the only love which has lasted is the love which has everything, every disappointment, every failure, and every betrayal, which has accepted even the sad fact that in the end there is no desire so deep as the simple desire for companionship.

—GRAHAM GREENE

WEDDING SONG

Now some people thinks it's jolly for to
lead a single life,
But I believe in marriage and the comforts
of a wife.
In fact you might have quarrels, just an
odd one now and then,
It's worth your while a-falling out to make
it up again.

—TRADITIONAL ENGLISH FOLK SONG

ANDREWS
AND
McMEEL
GIFT BOOKS

ISBN 0-8362-3007-8

9 780836 230079

50495

$4.95/$6.95 Canada

Jacket Design by
Beth Tondreau Design

Ariel Books

Andrews and McMeel

A Universal Press Syndicate Company

Kansas City

Printed in Hong Kong